CW00867600

SEA URCHINS
ARE BRAINLESS!

By Amanda Vink

Gareth Stevens
PUBLISHING

Please visit our website, www.garethstevens.com. For a free color catalog of all our high-quality books, call toll free 1-800-542-2595 or fax 1-877-542-2596.

Library of Congress Cataloging-in-Publication Data

Names: Vink, Amanda, author.
Title: Sea urchins are brainless! / Amanda Vink.
Description: New York : Gareth Stevens Publishing, [2020] | Series: Animals
  without brains! | Includes index. | Summary: "Sea urchins don't have brains! This text explores body
  parts sea urchins use instead, including an interior water pump that allows the creatures to move
  about and hold on to food."– Provided by publisher.
Identifiers: LCCN 2019027296 | ISBN 9781538246009 (library binding) | ISBN
  9781538245989 (paperback) | ISBN 9781538245996 | ISBN 9781538246016
  (ebook)
Subjects: LCSH: Sea urchins–Juvenile literature.
Classification: LCC QL384.E2 V56 2020 | DDC 593.9/5–dc23
LC record available at https://lccn.loc.gov/2019027296

Published in 2020 by
Gareth Stevens Publishing
111 East 14th Street, Suite 349
New York, NY 10003

Designer: Sarah Liddell
Editor: Amanda Vink

Photo credits: Cover, p. 1 HotFlash/Shutterstock.com; background used throughout Sanjatosic/
Shutterstock.com; p. 5 NatalieJean/Shutterstock.com; p. 7 Brandon B/Shutterstock.com;
p. 9 natfu/Shutterstock.com; p. 11 JGA/Shutterstock.com; p. 13 Valsib/Shutterstock.com;
p. 15 Greg Amptman/Shutterstock.com; p. 17 metha1819/Shutterstock.com; p. 19 Krzysztof
Bargiel/Shutterstock.com; p. 21 RelentlessImages/Shutterstock.com.

Printed in the United States of America

Some of the images in this book illustrate individuals who are models. The depictions do
not imply actual situations or events.

CPSIA compliance information: Batch #CW20GS: For further information contact Gareth Stevens, New York, New York at 1-800-542-2595.

CONTENTS

Boldface words appear in the glossary.

Brainless!

Sea urchins are invertebrates, or members of the **animal kingdom** that don't have a backbone or bony **skeleton**. Invertebrates make up 97 percent of all creatures! Many of these don't have brains, including sea urchins. How do sea urchins live without a brain?

Sea Hedgehogs

Sea urchins' bodies have a rounded shell with **radial symmetry**. Sticking out from the shell are sharp, moveable spines. Some people have nicknamed them sea hedgehogs! Roughly 200 species, or kinds, of sea urchins live in oceans all around the world.

Take A Bite

Sea urchins come in different sizes and colors. Their mouth is on the underside of the body. Sea urchins have a structure similar to teeth called an Aristotle's lantern. They use it to **scrape** algae and other food from rocks.

MOUTH

The Brainless Hunter

Sea urchins are **omnivores**. They eat seaweed, algae, and plankton, or tiny sea plants and animals. Without brains, they need a way to find **prey**! Sea urchins don't have eyes, but they can still "see" by taking in light around them.

The Nerve Net

Sea urchins have a simple nervous system, which helps them receive and respond to information in the world. A nerve net throughout the body holds cells that react to movement and light. These cells act like one big eye.

Moving About

Sea urchins rely on a water **vascular system**. They pump water through their bodies through an opening called a madreporite, which helps them breathe. This also allows sea urchins to move by filling and unfilling the tube feet located all over their bodies.

15

Protection

The long spiny needles on sea urchins offer them **protection**. Most stings to humans are painful, but not deadly. Some sea urchins, like the flower urchin found in the Indian and Pacific Oceans, have spines that hold **toxins**.

FLOWER URCHIN

17

Inside Out

A sea urchin sends millions of eggs into the water. Tiny larvae grow. When they're ready, they pull themselves inside out to become adults! Adult sea urchins can live for many years if they don't get eaten or sick.

A Balancing Act

Sea urchins play an important role in balancing the amount of coral and algae within an **ecosystem**. Many things affect sea urchin numbers, including humans eating them. Sea urchins may be brainless, but they've got an important job to do!

GLOSSARY

animal kingdom: a basic group of natural objects that includes all living and extinct animals

ecosystem: all the living things in an area

omnivore: an animal that eats both meat and plants

prey: an animal that is hunted by other animals for food

protection: the act of shielding from harm

radial symmetry: having similar parts arranged around a central point

scrape: to remove by repeated strokes with something sharp or rough

skeleton: the bony frame of the body

toxins: a poison produced by a living thing

vascular system: a system for the movement of a body fluid throughout the body

FOR MORE INFORMATION

BOOKS

Magby, Meryl. *Under the Sea: Sea Urchins*. New York, New York: PowerKids Press, 2013.

Quinlan, Julia. *Let's Find Out! Marine Life: What Are Sea Invertebrates?* New York, New York: Britannica Educational Publishing, 2017.

WEBSITES

Ducksters: Invertebrates
www.ducksters.com/animals/invertebrates.php
Visit this website to learn more about classifying invertebrates.

Kidzone: Animal Classes
www.kidzone.ws/animals/animal_classes.htm
To learn more about how scientists classify different animals, check out this site!

INDEX